sensational **sushi**

sensational sushi

stylish · healthy · fast

yasuko fukuoka

BARNES &NOBLE
BOOKS
NEW YORK

This edition published by Barnes & Noble, Inc.,
by arrangement with Anness Publishing Limited

2003 Barnes & Noble Books

ISBN 0-7607- 5036-X

M 10 9 8 7 6 5 4 3 2 1

A CIP catalogue record for this book is available from the
British Library.

PUBLISHER: Joanna Lorenz
MANAGING EDITOR: Linda Fraser
SENIOR EDITOR: Margaret Malone
DESIGNER: Luise Roberts
PHOTOGRAPHER: Craig Robertson
HOME ECONOMIST: Julie Beresford
STYLIST: Helen Trent
PRODUCTION CONTROLLER: Claire Rae
EDITORIAL READER: Joy Wotton

Printed in China

NOTES
Standard spoon and cup measures are level.
Large eggs are used unless otherwise stated.

contents

introduction

THE PROLIFERATION OF Japanese sushi bars in cities the world over has led to an enormous interest in these delectable morsels, which can be served as snacks or elegant dinner-party fare. Sushi consists of vinegared rice with a filling or topping that not only complements its flavor, but also looks exquisite. This might be vegetables or pickles, but is more often fresh raw fish. When the fish is served solo or in a salad, either raw or lightly cooked and skillfully cut into delicate wedges or paper-thin slices, it is called sashimi.

A professional sushi chef trains for many years, but don't let this put you off. A complete novice can master simple sushi-making in minutes. It doesn't matter if first attempts aren't perfect; making sushi and sashimi is fun, and even less artistic offerings will taste delicious.

SUSHI AND RICE DISHES

RICE IS AT THE HEART of Japanese cooking, and sushi is undoubtedly that nation's best-known rice dish. The most familiar version, *hoso-maki*, involves laying *su-meshi* (vinegared rice) on a sheet of *nori* seaweed and rolling it around one or more ingredients before slicing it into rolls. The rice can also be compressed into blocks and topped with fresh or smoked fish, as in *oshi-zushi*, or shaped by hand and coated in sesame seeds to make *onigiri*. The results are always exciting, elegant and easy on the eye. Turn to the back of the book for step-by-step instructions for making and shaping vinegared rice.

tamaki-zushi

THIS IS A FUN WAY TO ENJOY SUSHI. FILLINGS OF SEAFOOD, VEGETABLES AND *SU-MESHI* ARE ROLLED TOGETHER BY EACH GUEST TO MAKE DECORATIVE LITTLE SNACKS.

SERVES FOUR TO SIX

2 quantities of *su-meshi* (vinegared rice), made with 8 teaspoons superfine sugar in total
8 ounces very fresh tuna steak
4½ ounces smoked salmon
6½-inch Japanese cucumber or salad cucumber
8 raw jumbo shrimp, heads and shells removed, tails intact
1 avocado
1½ teaspoon lemon juice
20 chives cut into 2½-inch lengths
1 carton mustard and cress, roots cut off
6–8 *shiso* leaves, cut in half lengthwise

To serve

12 *nori* sheets, cut into tour
shoyu
3 tablespoons *wasabi* paste from a tube, or the same amount of *wasabi* powder mixed with 1 tablespoon water
gari

1   Put the *su-meshi* into a large serving bowl and cover with a damp dishtowel.

2   Slice the tuna, with the grain, into ¼-inch-thick slices, then into ½ x 2½-inch strips. Cut the salmon and cucumber into ½ x 2½-inch thin strips.

3   Insert small bamboo skewers lengthwise into the shrimp, then boil them in lightly salted water for 2 minutes. Drain and leave to cool, Remove the skewers and cut the shrimp in half lengthwise. Remove the vein. Halve the avocado and remove the pit. Sprinkle with half the lemon juice and cut into ½-inch-long strips. Sprinkle on the remaining lemon juice.

4   Arrange the fish, shrimp, avocado and herbs on a plate. Place the *nori* sheets on plates and put the *shoyu*, *wasabi* paste and *gari* in separate small bowls.

5   Each guest rolls their sushi as follows: take a sheet of *nori* on your palm, then scoop out 3 tablespoons rice and spread it on the *nori* sheet. Spread a little *wasabi* in the middle of the rice, then place a few strips of different fillings on top. Roll it up into a cone and dip the end into the *shoyu*, then eat. Eat a few slices of *gari* between rolls to refresh your mouth.

futo-maki

THERE ARE TWO MAIN TYPES OF *NORI-MAKI* OR ROLLED SUSHI: *FUTO-MAKI* AND *HOSO-MAKI* (NEXT PAGE). *FUTO-MAKI* MEANS "BIG ROLL", AND CONTAINS SEVERAL INGREDIENTS.

1 First make the omelette. Mix the beaten eggs, *dashi* stock, sake and salt in a bowl. Heat a little oil in a frying pan on a medium-low heat. Pour in just enough egg mixture to cover the base of the pan thinly. As soon as the mixture sets, fold the omelette in half toward you and wipe the space left with a little oil. With the first omelette still in the pan, repeat this process until all the mixture is used. Each new omelette is laid onto the first to form a multi-layered omelette. Slide the layered omelette onto a chopping board. Leave to cool, then cut lengthwise into ½-inch-wide strips.

2 Put the shiitake and the water, stock, *shoyu*, sugar and *mirin* in a small pan. Bring to the boil, then reduce the heat to low. Cook for 20 minutes until half of the liquid has evaporated. Drain the shiitake, remove and discard the stalks, and slice the caps thinly. Squeeze out any excess liquid, then dry on kitchen paper. Discard the liquid.

3 Make three cuts in the belly of each of the shrimp to stop them curling up, and boil in salted water for 1 minute, or until they turn bright pink. Drain and cool, then remove the vein.

4 Place a *nori* sheet, rough side up, at the front edge of the *makisu* (sushi rolling mat). Scoop up half of the *su-meshi* and spread it on the *nori*. Leave a ½-inch margin at the side nearest you, and ¾ inch at the side furthest from you. Make a shallow depression lengthwise across the center of the rice. Fill this with half the omelette strips and half the asparagus. Place half the shrimp along the egg and asparagus. Top with 5 chives and half the the shiitake slices.

5 Lift the *makisu* with your thumbs while pressing the filling with your fingers. Roll the *makisu* up gently. When completed, gently roll the *makisu* to firm it up. Unwrap and set the *futo-maki* aside. Repeat to make another roll. Serve as for *hoso-maki* (next page). ▶

Left: A platter of *nori-maki*. The larger *futo-maki* are in the foreground, with *hoso-maki* behind.

MAKES SIXTEEN ROLLS

2 *nori* sheets
1 quantity of *su-meshi* (vinegared rice)

For the omelette
2 eggs, beaten
1½ tablespoons second *dashi* stock
2 teaspoons sake
½ teaspoon salt
vegetable oil, for frying

For the fillings
4 dried shiitake mushrooms, soaked in water overnight
4 fluid ounces | ½ cup second *dashi* stock
1 tablespoon *shoyu*
1½ teaspoons sugar
1 teaspoon *mirin*
6 raw jumbo shrimp, heads and shells removed
4 asparagus spears, boiled for 1 minute in lightly salted water, cooled
10 chives, about 9 inches long

hoso-maki

MAKES TWENTY-FOUR ROLLS

2 *nori* sheets, cut in half crosswise
1 quantity of *su-meshi*
    (vinegared rice) divided into
    four equal amounts
3 tablespoons *wasabi* paste from
    a tube, or the same amount of
    wasabi powder mixed with
    2 teaspoons water

For the fillings

3½ ounces very fresh tuna steak
4-inch salad cucumber or 6½-inch
    Japanese cucumber, cut into
    ½-inch-thick long strips
1 teaspoon toasted sesame seeds
2¼-inch *takuan*, cut into
    ½-inch-thick long strips

To serve

2 tablespoons rice vinegar
4 teaspoons *wasabi* paste from
    a tube, or 1 tablespoon
    wasabi powder mixed with
    1½ teaspoons water
gari
shoyu

1   To make the *hoso-maki*, cut the tuna with the grain into ½-inch-wide strips. Half-fill a small mixing bowl with water and add a little rice vinegar. Use this to wet your hands when rolling the sushi.

2   Place the *makisu* (sushi rolling mat) on the work surface, then place a *nori* sheet on it horizontally, rough side up. Spread a quarter of the *su-meshi* over the *nori* to cover evenly, leaving a ½-inch margin on the side farthest from you. Press firmly to smooth the surface.

3   Spread a very little *wasabi* paste across the center of the rice and arrange some tuna strips horizontally in a row. Trim the tuna ends neatly.

4   Hold the *makisu* with both hands and roll it up from the side closest to you toward the other side, wrapping the tuna in the middle. Hold the rolled *makisu* with both hands and squeeze gently to firm the *hoso-maki*. Gently unwrap the *makisu* and transfer the sushi to a slightly damp chopping board. Cover with plastic wrap. (As you complete each rolled sushi, transfer it to the board and cover.) Make another tuna *hoso-maki* with the remaining ingredients.

5   Repeat the process with another sheet of *nori* and a quarter of the rice, using the cucumber sticks with green skin. Sprinkle sesame seeds on the cucumber before rolling.

6   Make one more with the *takuan* sticks, but omitting the *wasabi* paste. You should have 2 *hoso-maki* of tuna, and 1 each of cucumber and *takuan*.

cook's tip
Try to place the ingredients right in the middle of the rice, so that they stay in the center when the *nori* and rice are rolled up.

stylish serving suggestions

Cut each *hoso-maki* roll crosswise into six pieces, and each *futo-maki roll* into eight pieces. Use a very sharp knife and wipe it with a dishtowel dampened with rice vinegar after each cut. Line up the sushi on a large tray. Serve with small dishes of *wasabi*, *gari* and *shoyu* for dipping.

oshi-zushi

THIS SIMPLE RECIPE OF COMPRESSED SUSHI WITH SMOKED SALMON DATES BACK ALMOST A THOUSAND YEARS. IF YOU HAVEN'T MADE SUSHI BEFORE, THIS IS A GOOD RECIPE TO START WITH.

MAKES ABOUT TWELVE

6 ounces smoked salmon,
    thickly sliced
1 tablespoon sake
1 tablespoon water
2 tablespoons *shoyu*
1 quantity of *su-meshi*
    (vinegared rice)
2 tablespoons rice vinegar
1 lemon, thinly sliced into
    ¼-inch rings and quartered

1 Lay the smoked salmon on a chopping board and sprinkle with a mixture of the sake, water and *shoyu*. Leave to marinate for an hour, then wipe dry with paper towels.

2 Wet a wooden Japanese mold or line a 10 x 3 x 2-inch container with a sheet of plastic wrap twice the size of the container.

3 Spread half the salmon to cover the base of the container. Add a quarter of the rice and press down with your hands dampened with rice vinegar until it is ½ inch thick. Add the remainder of the salmon, press the remaining rice on top.

4 Cover with the wet wooden lid or the hanging plastic wrap. Place a weight, such as a heavy dinner plate, on top. Leave in a cool place for at least 3 hours. If you keep it in the refrigerator, choose the least cool part, such as the top shelf.

5 Remove the compressed sushi from the mold or container and unwrap. Cut into ¾-inch slices and serve on a Japanese lacquered tray or a large plate. Top each piece with 2 slices of lemon and serve.

saba-zushi

MACKEREL IS MARINATED AND PACKED INTO A MOLD WITH *SU-MESHI* TO MAKE A DELICIOUS APPETIZER. START PREPARING 8 HOURS IN ADVANCE TO ALLOW THE FISH TO ABSORB THE SALT.

1 Place the mackerel fillets skin-side down in a flat dish, cover with a thick layer of salt, and leave them for 3–5 hours in the refrigerator.

2 Wipe the salt from the mackerel with paper towels. Remove all the remaining bones with tweezers. Lift the skin at the tail end of each fillet and gently peel off toward the head end. Place the skinned fillets in a clean dish, and pour in enough rice vinegar to cover the fish completely. Leave for 20 minutes, then drain and wipe dry with paper towels.

3 Line a 10 x 3 x 1½-inch container with a sheet of plastic wrap, twice the size of the container. Lay all but 1 of the mackerel fillets in the container, skinned side down, to cover the base. Cut the remaining mackerel fillet to fill the gaps.

4 Put the *su-meshi* on top of the mackerel in the container, and press down firmly with dampened hands. Cover with the plastic wrap and place a weight on top. Leave in a cool place for at least 3 hours or overnight.

5 Remove the sushi from its container, then slice crosswise into ¾-inch pieces. After cutting each slice, wipe the knife with a paper towel dampened with rice vinegar. Arrange the sushi on a plate and garnish each piece with a little grated ginger. Serve with *shoyu*.

MAKES ABOUT TWELVE

1¼ pounds mackerel, filleted
rice vinegar
1 quantity of *su-meshi*
   (vinegared rice)
¾-inch ginger root, peeled and
   finely grated, to garnish
shoyu, to serve
salt

nigiri-zushi

ORIGINALLY DEVELOPED IN TOKYO AS STREET-FINGER FOOD, HAND-MOLDED SUSHI IS PREPARED
WITH THE FRESHEST OF FISH AND EATEN WITHIN A FEW HOURS OF MAKING.

SERVES FOUR

4 raw jumbo shrimp, heads and
    shells removed, tails intact
4 scallops, white muscle only
15 ounces assorted fresh fish, such
    as tuna, salmon, sea bass and
    mackerel, skinned, cleaned
    and filleted
2 quantities of *su-meshi*
    (vinegared rice)
1 tablespoon rice vinegar,
    for moulding
3 tablespoons *wasabi* paste from
    a tube, or the same amount
    of *wasabi* powder mixed with
    1 tablespoon water
salt
shoyu and *gari*, to serve

1 Insert a short bamboo skewer into each shrimp lengthwise. This stops the shrimp
curling up when cooked. Boil them in lightly salted water for 2 minutes, or until they turn
pink. Drain and cool, then pull out the skewers. Cut open from the belly side but do not
slice in two. With the point of a sharp knife, scoop up the black vein running down its
length. Very gently pull it out, then discard. Open out flat and place on a tray.

2 Slice the scallops horizontally in half, but not quite through. Gently open each scallop
at this "hinge" to make a butterfly shape. Place on the tray, cut-side down. Use a very
sharp knife to cut all the fish fillets into 3 x 1½ inch pieces, ¼ inch thick. Place all the raw
fish and shellfish on the tray, cover with plastic wrap, then chill.

3 Place the *su-meshi* in a bowl. Have ready a small bowl filled with ¼ pint|⅔ cup water
and the vinegar for molding. This water is used for your hands while making *nigiri-zushi*.
Take the tray of toppings from the refrigerator.

4 Wash your hands with unperfumed soap and rinse well. Wet them with the vinegared
water and scoop about 1½ tablespoons *su-meshi* into your palm. Gently but firmly grip
the *su-meshi* and make a rectangular block. Do not squash the rice block, but ensure
that the grains stick together. The size of the blocks must be smaller than the toppings.

5 Put the *su-meshi* block on a damp chopping board. Taking a piece of topping in your
palm, rub a little *wasabi* paste in the middle of it. Put the *su-meshi* block on top of the
topping and gently press it. Form your palm into a cup and shape the *nigiri-zushi* into a
smooth-surfaced mound. Place it on a serving tray. Do not overwork the sushi, as the
warmth of your hands can cause the toppings to lose their freshness.

6 Repeat this process until all of the rice and toppings are used. Serve immediately with
a little *shoyu* dribbled on individual plates. To eat, pick up a *nigiri-zushi* and dip one end
into the *shoyu*. Eat a little *gari* between different sushi to refresh your mouth.

onigiri

MEANING HAND-MOLDED RICE, THESE TASTY RICE BALLS ARE FILLED WITH SALMON, MACKEREL, *UMEBOSHI* OR OLIVES. THE *NORI* COATING MAKES THEM EASY TO PICK UP WITH YOUR FINGERS.

1 To cook the rice, wash it thoroughly with cold water. Drain and put into a heavy pan. Pour in the water and leave for 30 minutes. Put the lid on tightly and bring to the boil. Reduce the heat and simmer for 12 minutes. You should hear a crackling noise from the rice, remove the pan from the heat and leave to stand, covered, for about 15 minutes.

2 Stir the rice carefully with a dampened wooden spatula to aerate it. Leave to cool for 30 minutes. Thoroughly salt the salmon fillet and leave for at least 30 minutes.

3 Pit the *umeboshi*. With the back of a fork, mash them slightly. Mix with 1 tablespoon of the sesame seeds and the *mirin* to make a rough paste.

4 Wash the salt from the salmon. Broil the salmon and smoked mackerel under a high heat until cooked. Using a fork, remove the skin from the mackerel and divide the fish into loose, chunky flakes. Keep the salmon and mackerel pieces separate.

5 Dry-fry the remaining sesame seeds in a heavy dry frying pan over a low heat until they start to pop.
▶

SERVES FOUR

2 ounces salmon fillet, skinned
3 *umeboshi*, 2 ounces in
   total weight
3 tablespoons sesame seeds
½ teaspoon *mirin*
2 ounces smoked mackerel fillet
2 *nori* sheets, each cut into 6 strips
6 pitted black olives, wiped and
   finely chopped
fine salt
Japanese pickles, to serve

For the rice

1 pound | 2¼ cups Japanese short
   grain rice
18 fluid ounces | 2½ cups water

6   Check the temperature of the rice. It should be still quite warm but not hot. To start molding, you will need a teacup and a tablespoon, plus a bowl of cold water to wet your hands. Put the teacup and tablespoon into the water. Put some fine salt into a small dish. Wipe a chopping board with a very wet dishtowel. Wash your hands thoroughly with unperfumed soap and rinse well.

7   Remove the cup and spoon from the bowl and shake off excess water. Scoop about 2 tablespoons rice into the teacup. With your fingers, make a well in the center of the rice and put in a quarter of the salmon flakes. Cover with 1 tablespoon rice and press well.

8   Wet your hands and sprinkle them with a pinch of salt. Rub it all over your palms. Turn the rice in the teacup out into one hand and squeeze the rice shape with both hands to make a densely packed flat ball.

9   Wrap the rice ball with a *nori* strip, seal with a grain of rice and transfer to the chopping board. Make three more balls using the remaining salmon, then make four balls using the smoked mackerel and another four balls using the *umeboshi* paste.

10   Scoop about 3 tablespoons rice into the teacup. Mix in a quarter of the chopped olives. Press the rice with your fingers. Wet your hands with water and rub with a pinch of salt and a quarter of the toasted sesame seeds. Turn the teacup onto one hand and shape the rice mixture into a ball as above. The sesame seeds should stick to the rice. This time, do not wrap with *nori*. Repeat, making three more balls. Serve one of each kind of rice ball on individual plates with a small helping of Japanese pickles to accompany.

rice triangles

As an alternative, shape the rice into pretty triangles. Use both hands to shape the rice into a triangular shape, using firm but not heavy pressure. Wrap a *nori* strip around the triangles of rice containing the salmon, mackerel and *umeboshi* balls, as before. Coat the olive and rice triangles with alternating white and black sesame seeds.

chirashi

JEWEL BOX SUSHI IS THE MOST COMMON FORM OF SUSHI EATEN AT HOME IN JAPAN. A LACQUERED CONTAINER IS FILLED WITH *SU-MESHI*, AND INGREDIENTS ARE ARRANGED ON TOP.

SERVES FOUR

2 eggs, beaten
vegetable oil, for frying
2 ounces snow peas, trimmed
1 *nori* sheet
1 tablespoon *shoyu*
1 tablespoon *wasabi* paste from a
  tube, or the same amount of
  wasabi powder mixed with
  2 teaspoons water
1¼ quantities of *su-meshi*
  (vinegared rice) made with
  40ml|8 teaspoon sugar
2–4 tablespoons *ikura*, to garnish
salt

**For the fish and shellfish
toppings**
4 ounces very fresh tuna steak,
  skin removed
3½ ounces fresh squid, body only
4 raw jumbo shrimp, heads and
  shells removed, tails intact

For the marinated shiitake
8 dried shiitake mushrooms,
  soaked in 12 fluid ounces|
  1½ cups water for 4 hours
1 tablespoon superfine sugar
4 tablespoons *mirin*
3 tablespoons *shoyu*

1   Slice the tuna across the grain into 3 x 1½-inch pieces, ¼-inch thick. Slice the squid crosswise into ¼-inch strips. Place all on a tray, cover and chill.

2   Meanwhile, prepare the marinated shiitake: remove and discard the stalks from the soaked shiitake. Pour the soaking water into a pan, add the shiitake and bring to the boil. Skim the surface and reduce the heat. Cook for 20 minutes, then add the sugar. Reduce the heat to low and add the *mirin* and *shoyu*. Simmer until almost all the liquid has evaporated. Drain the mushrooms and slice very thinly. Set aside.

3   Insert a short bamboo skewer into each shrimp lengthwise. Boil in salted water for 2 minutes. Drain and leave to cool.

4   Remove the skewers from the shrimp. Cut open from the belly side but do not slice in two. Remove the black vein. Open the shrimp out flat and add to the tray.

5   Beat the eggs in a bowl with a pinch of salt. Heat a little oil in a frying pan until it smokes. Wipe away the excess oil with a paper towel. Add enough beaten egg to cover the bottom of the pan thinly. Cook on a medium-low heat until the edge is dry and starting to curl. Lift the omelette and turn over. After 30 seconds, place on a chopping board. Repeat to make several omelettes. Roll them together into a tube and slice very thinly.

6   Par-boil the snow peas for 2 minutes in lightly salted water, drain. Cut into ⅛-inch diagonal strips. Snip the *nori* into fine shreds. Mix with the *shoyu* and *wasabi*.

7   Divide half the *su-meshi* among four bowls or containers. Spread a quarter of the *nori* mixture over each. Cover with the rest of the *su-meshi*. Flatten the surface with a wet spatula. Sprinkle over the omelette strands to cover the surface. Arrange the tuna in a fan shape with a fan of shiitake on top. Place a shrimp next to the tuna, and arrange the squid strips on the other side. Top with the snow peas and *ikura*.

inari-zushi

ABURA-AGE IS DIFFERENT TO OTHER TOFU PRODUCTS, AS IT CAN BE OPENED UP LIKE A BAG. HERE IT'S COOKED IN SOY-SAUCE-BASED SEASONINGS AND FILLED WITH *SU-MESHI*.

1 Par-boil the fresh *abura-age* in rapidly boiling water for about 1 minute. Drain, then rinse under running water and leave to cool. Gently squeeze out the excess water. Cut each piece of *abura-age* in half crosswise and carefully pull open the cut end to make bags. If you are using canned *abura-age*, drain the liquid.

2 Lay the *abura-age* bags in a large pan. Pour in the *dashi* stock to cover and bring to the boil. Reduce the heat and cover, then simmer for 20 minutes. Add the sugar in three batches during this time, shaking the pan to dissolve it. Simmer for a further 15 minutes. Add the sake. Shake the pan again, and add the *shoyu* in three batches. Simmer until almost all the liquid has evaporated. Transfer the *abura-age* to a wide strainer and leave to drain.

3 Mix the *su-meshi* and sesame seeds in a wet mixing bowl. Wet your hands and take a little *su-meshi*. Shape it into a rectangular block. Open one *abura-age* bag and insert the *su-meshi* block. Press the edges together to close the bag.

4 Once all the bags have been filled, place them on a large serving plate or individual plates with the bottom of the bag on top. Garnish with a little *gari*.

SERVES FOUR

8 fresh *abura-age* (fried thin tofu) or 10-ounce can ready-to-use *abura-age* (contains 16 halves)
1½ pints | 3¾ cups second *dashi* stock, or the same amount of water and 2 teaspoons *dashi-no-moto*
6 tablespoons superfine sugar
2 tablespoons sake
4½ tablespoons *shoyu*
generous 1 quantity *su-meshi* (vinegared rice), made with 8 teaspoons sugar
2 tablespoons toasted sesame seeds
gari, to garnish

cook's tip

To open the *abura-age* without breaking them, place them on a chopping board and with the palm of your hand, rub them gently on the board. Then pull apart little by little from the cut end and work towards the bottom. When fully open, put your finger inside and make sure the corners are opened completely.

sekihan

THIS STICKY RED RICE DISH IS COOKED FOR SPECIAL OCCASIONS AND TAKES 8 HOURS TO PREPARE. EDIBLE *KASHIWA* (SALTED OAK) LEAVES ARE TRADITIONALLY USED FOR A BOY-CHILD'S FESTIVAL.

SERVES FOUR

2½ ounces | ½ cup dried
    adzuki beans
1 teaspoon salt
11 ounces | 1½ cups *mochigome*
    (Japanese glutinous rice)
2 ounces | ¼ cup Japanese short
    grain rice
12 *kashiwa* (salted oak) leaves
    (optional)

For the *goma-shio* (sesame salt)

3 tablespoons sesame seeds
    (black sesame if available)
1 teaspoon ground sea salt

1 Put the beans in a heavy pan and add 15 fluid ounces | 1¾ cups of water. Bring to the boil, reduce the heat and gently simmer, covered, for 20–30 minutes. Remove the pan from the heat and drain. Reserve the cooking liquid. Return the beans to the pan and add the salt.

2 Wash the two rices together. Drain in a strainer and leave for 30 minutes.

3 Bring another 15 fluid ounces | 1¾ cups of water to the boil. Add to the beans and bring to the boil, then simmer for 30 minutes. When the beans' skins start to crack, drain them. Add the liquid to the reserved liquid. Cover the beans and leave to cool.

4 Add the rice to the bean liquid. Leave to soak for 4–5 hours. Drain the rice and reserve the liquid. Mix the beans into the rice.

5 Bring a steamer of water to the boil. Turn off the heat. Place a tall glass upside down in the center of the steaming compartment. Pour the rice and beans into the steamer and gently pull the glass out. The hole in the middle will allow even distribution of the steam. Steam over a high heat for 10 minutes.

6 Sprinkle the rice with the reserved liquid. Cover and repeat twice more at 10-minute intervals. Steam for 15 minutes more. Remove from the heat and stand for 10 minutes.

7 Make the *goma-shio*. Roast the sesame seeds and salt in a dry frying pan until the seeds start to pop. Leave to cool, then put in a small dish.

8 Wipe each leaf with a wet dishtowel. Scoop 4 fluid ounces | ½ cup of the rice mixture into a wet teacup and press with wet fingers. Turn the cup upside down and shape the molded rice into a flat ball. Insert into a leaf folded in two. Repeat until all the leaves are used. Alternately, transfer the rice to a bowl wiped with a wet dishtowel. Serve with *goma-shio*.

san-shoku bento

THIS IS A TYPICAL *BENTO* (LUNCH BOX) MENU FOR JAPANESE CHILDREN. COLORFUL TOPPINGS AND A VARIETY OF TASTES HOLD THEIR ATTENTION SO THEY DON'T GET BORED.

1 To make the *iri-tamago*, add the sugar and salt to the eggs in a pan. Cook over a medium heat, stirring with a whisk or a fork as you would to scramble egg. When it is almost set, remove from the heat and stir until the egg becomes fine and slightly dry.

2 To make the *denbu*, cook the cod fillet for 2 minutes in a large pan of boiling water. Drain and dry well with a paper towel. Skin and remove all the fish bones.

3 Put the cod and sugar into a pan, add the salt and sake, and cook over a low heat for 1 minute, stirring with a fork to flake the cod. Reduce the heat to low and sprinkle over the coloring. Continue to stir for 15–20 minutes, or until the cod flakes become very fluffy and fibrous. Transfer the denbu to a plate.

4 To make the *tori-soboro*, put the minced chicken, sake, sugar, shoyu and water into a pan. Cook over a medium heat for 3 minutes, then reduce the heat to medium-low and stir with a fork or whisk until the liquid has almost evaporated.

5 Blanch the snow peas for about 3 minutes in lightly salted boiling water, drain and carefully slice into fine ⅛-inch sticks.

6 Mix the rice with the sesame seeds in a bowl. With a wet spoon, divide the rice among four 6½ x 4½-inch lunch boxes. Flatten the surface of the rice using the back of a wooden spoon.

7 Spoon a quarter of the egg into each box to cover a third of the rice. Cover the next third with a quarter of the *denbu*, and the last section with a quarter of the *tori-soboro* topping. Use the lid to divide the boxes, if you like. Garnish with the snow pea sticks.

MAKES FOUR LUNCH BOXES

3 snow peas
10 ounces | scant 1½ cups
    Japanese short grain rice
    cooked using 13 fluid ounces |
    scant 1⅔ cups water, cooled
3 tablespoons sesame seeds,
    toasted
salt

For the *iri-tamago*
  (yellow topping)
2 tablespoons superfine sugar
1 teaspoon salt
3 eggs, beaten

For the *denbu* (pink topping)
4 ounces cod fillet, skinned
    and boned
4 teaspoons superfine sugar
1 teaspoon salt
1 teaspoon sake
2 drops of red vegetable coloring,
    diluted with a little water

For the *tori-soboro*
  (beige topping)
7 ounces ground raw chicken
3 tablespoons sake
1 tablespoon superfine sugar
1 tablespoon shoyu
1 tablespoon water

SASHIMI

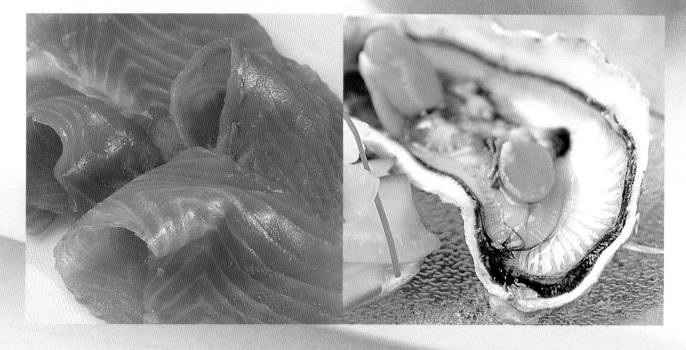

THE POPULAR CONCEPTION of sashimi as raw fish is accurate enough, but such a bald description cannot convey the delicacy of its flavor, nor the artistry with which it is presented. Some types of fish are shaved into paper-thin slices, while others are cut in chunks or finger-width pieces. Nor is the fish necessarily raw; it can be marinated in lemon juice or vinegar, seared briefly or blanched for a few seconds. Sashimi can be served solo, with a little *wasabi* and *shoyu*, but it also tastes superb in salads.

sashimi moriawase

THE FRESHNESS AND THE ARRANGEMENT OF THE FISH ARE THE TWO MOST IMPORTANT FACTORS IN ANY SASHIMI. FOR THIS DISH, CHOOSE TWO TO FIVE KINDS OF FISH FROM EACH GROUP.

1 Make the *tsuma* (daikon strands). Slice the daikon very thinly lengthwise then cut the slices into very thin strips lengthwise. Rinse under running water, then drain and chill.

2 Slice the fish. Group A needs *hira giri*, a thick cut: trim the fillet into a long rectangular shape. Place on a chopping board horizontally, skinned side up. Using a very sharp knife, cut into ½-inch-thick slices along the grain.

3 Group B needs *usu zukuri*, very thin slices. Place the fillet horizontally on its skinned side. Hold the knife almost horizontally to the fillet, shave it thinly across the grain.

4 Group C fish each require different cutting styles. Cut open the squid body and turn it to lie on its skinned side. Score lines ¼ inch apart lengthwise all over the surface of the squid, then cut it into ¼ inch-thick strips.

5 Slice the cooked octopus diagonally into ¼-inch-thick ovals. Finely slice the scallops in half horizontally. If they are thicker than 1½ inches, slice each one into three. Group D is ready to arrange on the serving plates. ▶

SERVES FOUR

1½ pounds total of fish from the 4 groups

Group A, skinned fillets (cut lengthwise if possible)
maguro akami (lean tuna)
maguro toro (fatty tuna)
sake (salmon)
me-kajiki (swordfish)
tai (red snapper)
suzuki (sea bream)
hamachi (yellowtail)
katsuo (bonito)

Group B, skinned fillets
hirame (flounder or sole)
karei (plaice or turbot)

Group C
ika (squid), body only, cleaned, boned and skinned
tako (cooked octopus tentacles)
hotate-gai (scallop), the coral, black stomach and frill removed

Group D
ebi (prawn), peeled, heads can be removed, tails intact
uni (sea urchin)
ikura (salted salmon roe)

To serve

1 fresh daikon, peeled and cut into
   2½-inch lengths
4 *shiso* leaves
1 Japanese or salad cucumber,
   trimmed and cut into
   1¼-inch lengths
3 tablespoons *wasabi* paste from
   a tube, or the same amount of
   wasabi powder mixed with
   4 teaspoons water
1 bottle *tamari shoyu*

6   Arrange the sashimi creatively. First, take a handful of daikon strands and heap on a *shiso* leaf or directly onto the serving plate to create a large mound or several small mounds. Then, base your design on the following basic rules:

Group A and C Put each slice of fish side by side like domino pieces. You can lay them on a *shiso* leaf.

Group B Use these thin, soft slices of fish to make a rose shape, or overlap the slices slightly, so that the texture of the plate can be seen through them.

Group D Arrange the shrimp on the plate or place them, 2–3 at a time, in a bundle. If the sea urchins come tightly packed in a little box, try to get them out in one piece; use a metal spatula to do this. The salmon roe can be arranged in a row or heaped on thin cucumber slices.

7   Make the cucumber fans. Cut the cucumber cylinders in half lengthwise. Place one on a chopping board, flat-side down. Make a series of very fine cuts across it, leaving the slices joined together at one side, then, gently squeeze the cucumber together between your fingers so that the slices fan out sideways.

8   Arrange the cucumber fans, heaped *wasabi* paste and *shiso* leaves to perfect your design. Serve immediately. Pour some *tamari shoyu* into four small dishes and mix in the *wasabi* paste for dipping. As the sauce is quite salty, dip only the edge of the sashimi into it before eating.

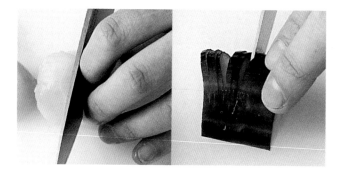

elegant presentation

Add height to the arrangement on the serving plate by spearing a shrimp or propping it so that it stands upright. If preparing this dish for a party, serve the salmon roe in a lime case. Remove the flesh from half a lime, fill it with some daikon strands and place the roe on top.

hirame konbu jime to nama-gaki no salada

OYSTERS, FLAVORED WITH A RICE-VINEGAR DRESSING, TASTE WONDERFUL WITH LEMON SOLE
SASHIMI. YOU'LL NEED TO START PREPARATIONS FOR THIS DISH AT LEAST 4 HOURS IN ADVANCE.

SERVES FOUR

1 very fresh lemon sole, skinned
   and filleted into 4
7 tablespoons rice vinegar
dashi-konbu, in 4 pieces, big
   enough to cover the fillets
2 ounces Japanese cucumber,
   ends trimmed, or ordinary salad
   cucumber with seeds removed
2 ounces celery, strings removed
2 pound large fava beans, podded
1 lime, ½ thinly sliced
4 tablespoons walnut oil
seeds from ½ pomegranate,
   optional
salt

For the oysters

1 tablespoon rice vinegar
2 tablespoons *shoyu*
1 tablespoon sake
12 large fresh oysters, opened
1 ounce daikon or radishes,
   peeled and very finely grated
8 chives, to garnish

1 Sprinkle salt on the sole fillets. Cover and chill for an hour.

2 Mix the rice vinegar and a similar amount of water in a bowl. Wash the fish fillets in the mixture, then drain thoroughly. Cut each fillet in half lengthwise.

3 Lay 1 piece of *dashi-konbu* on a work surface. Place a pair of sole fillets, skinned sides together, onto it, then lay another piece of *konbu* on top. Cover all the fillets like this and chill for 3 hours.

4 Halve the cucumber crosswise and slice thinly lengthwise. Then slice again diagonally into ¾-inch-wide pieces. Do the same for the celery. Sprinkle the cucumber with salt and leave to soften for 30–60 minutes. Gently squeeze to remove the moisture. Rinse if it tastes too salty, but drain well.

5 Boil the fava beans in lightly salted water for 15 minutes, or until soft. Drain and cool under running water, then peel off the skins. Sprinkle with salt.

6 Mix the rice vinegar, *shoyu* and sake for the oysters in a small bowl.

7 Slice the sole very thinly with a sharp knife. Remove the slightly chewy *dashi-konbu* first, if you prefer.

8 Place some pieces of cucumber and celery in a small mound in the center of four serving plates, then lay lime slices on top. Garnish with some chopped chives. Place the oysters to one side of the cucumber, topped with a few fava beans, then season with 1 teaspoon of the vinegar mix and 2 teaspoons grated daikon or radishes. Arrange the sole sashimi on the other side and drizzle walnut oil and a little lime juice on top. Add pomegranate seeds, if using, and serve.

kajiki no tataki salad

THIS DELICATE DISH MIXES JAPANESE COOKING TECHNIQUES WITH INTERNATIONAL INFLUENCES. FRESH FISH IS SLICED THINLY AND SEARED OR MARINATED, THEN SERVED WITH A TANGY CITRUS DRESSING.

1 Make the vegetable garnishes first. Use a very sharp knife, mandoline or vegetable slicer with a julienne blade to make very thin, about 1½-inch long strands of daikon, carrot and cucumber. Soak the daikon and carrot in ice-cold water for 5 minutes, then drain well and keep in the refrigerator.

2 Mix together all the ingredients for the dressing and stir well, then chill.

3 Heat the oil in a small frying pan until smoking. Sear the fish for 30 seconds on all sides. Plunge it into a bowl of cold water to stop it cooking. Dry on paper towels and wipe off as much oil as possible.

4 Cut the swordfish steak in half lengthwise before slicing it into ¼-inch-thick pieces in the other direction, against the grain.

5 Arrange the fish slices into a ring on 4 individual plates. Mix the vegetable strands, mustard and cress and sesame seeds. Fluff up with your hands, then shape them into four bundles. Gently place in the center of each ring of swordfish. Pour the dressing around the edge of the plates and serve immediately.

cook's tip
If you have a swordfish fillet cut with the grain, cut it in half lengthwise, then slice against the grain by holding a sharp knife almost horizontally to the chopping board.

SERVES FOUR

3 ounces daikon, peeled
2 ounces carrot, peeled
1 Japanese or salad cucumber
2 teaspoons vegetable oil
11 ounces skinned fresh swordfish steak, cut against the grain
2 cartons mustard and cress, roots cut off
1 tablespoon sesame seeds, toasted

For the dressing
7 tablespoons *shoyu*
7 tablespoons second *dashi* stock, or the same amount of water and 1 teaspoon *dashi-no-moto*
2 tablespoons toasted sesame oil
juice of ½ lime
rind of ½ lime, cut into thin strips

suzuki to ebi no o-sashimi salad

WHITE FISH IS BRIEFLY SEARED, THEN SERVED WITH SHRIMP AND SALAD IN AN OIL-FREE APRICOT AND APPLE DRESSING. THE FRUIT FLAVORS MAKE A DELICATE ACCOMPANIMENT TO THE FISH.

SERVES FOUR

1 young onion
dash of lemon juice
14 ounces very fresh sea bream
  or sea bass, filleted
2 tablespoons sake
4 large king jumbo shrimp,
  heads and shells removed
about 14 ounces mixed
  salad leaves

For the fruit dressing
2 ripe apricots, skinned and pitted
¼ apple, peeled and cored
4 tablespoons second *dashi* stock
  or the same amount of water
  and 1 teaspoon *dashi-no-moto*
2 teaspoons *shoyu*
salt and ground white pepper

1 Slice the onion thinly lengthwise, soak in ice-cold water for 30 minutes. Drain well.

2 Bring a pan half-full of water to the boil. Add a dash of lemon juice and plunge the fish fillets into it. Remove after 30 seconds, and cool immediately under cold running water for 30 seconds to stop them cooking. Cut crosswise into ⅜-inch-thick slices.

3 Pour the sake into a small pan, bring to the boil, then add the shrimp. Cook for 1 minute, or until their color has completely changed to pink. Cool immediately under cold running water for 30 seconds to again stop the cooking. Cut the shrimp crosswise into ½-inch-thick slices.

4 Slice 1 of the apricots very thinly, then set aside. Puree the other apricot with the rest of the dressing ingredients in a food processor. Add salt, if required, and pepper. Chill.

5 Lay a small amount of the salad leaves on each of four plates. Mix the fish, shrimp, apricot and onion slices in a bowl. Add the remaining leaves, then pour on the dressing and toss well. Heap up on the salad leaves on the plates and serve immediately.

hirame no o-sashimi salad

EATING SASHIMI WITH SAUCES, AN ANCIENT PRACTICE, ALMOST DISAPPEARED WHEN *SHOYU* BECAME POPULAR IN THE 17TH CENTURY. INTERESTINGLY, IT IS THROUGH WESTERN-INSPIRED SALADS, SUCH AS THIS ONE, THAT THEY HAVE REGAINED THEIR PLACE IN JAPANESE COOKING.

1 First make the dressing. Roughly tear apart the arugula leaves and process with the cucumber and rice vinegar in a food processor or blender until smooth. Pour into a small bowl and add the rest of the dressing ingredients, except for the *wasabi*. Check the seasoning and add more salt, if required. Chill until needed.

2 Prepare a bowl of cold water with a few ice cubes. Cut the turbot fillet in half lengthwise, then cut into ¼-inch-thick slices crosswise. Plunge these into the ice-cold water as you slice. After 2 minutes or so, they will start to curl and become firm. Take out and drain on kitchen paper.

3 In a large bowl, mix the fish, salad leaves and radishes. Mix the *wasabi* into the dressing, pour over the salad and toss well. Serve immediately.

cook's tips
- It is important to use Japanese rice vinegar. It has a mild, sweet aroma and is less sharp than Chinese rice vinegar. Though it has a wonderfully smooth flavor, avoid adding more than the amount specified, or it will overpower the other ingredients.
- If you can't buy turbot, brill, halibut, porgy or fillets of sole can be used instead.
- Chill the serving plates while you prepare the fish, if you like.

SERVES FOUR

ice cubes
14 ounces very fresh thick turbot, skinned and filleted
11 ounces mixed salad leaves
8 radishes, thinly sliced

For the wasabi dressing
1 ounce arugula leaves
2 ounces cucumber, chopped
6 tablespoons rice vinegar
5 tablespoons olive oil
1 teaspoon salt
1 tablespoon *wasabi* paste from a tube, or the same amount of *wasabi* powder mixed with 1½ teaspoons water

hotate kobachi

THE JAPANESE NAME FOR THIS DISH MEANS "SCALLOP IN A LITTLE DEEP BOWL". THIS IS A TYPICAL
SERVING SIZE AS A MEAL USUALLY CONSISTS OF AT LEAST THREE DISHES.

SERVES FOUR

8 scallops or 16 queen scallops,
    cleaned and coral removed
¼ dried sheet chrysanthemum
    petals or a handful of
    edible flower petals such
    as yellow nasturtium
4 bunches of watercress,
    leaves only

For the dressing

2 tablespoons *shoyu*, plus extra
    for serving
1 teaspoon sake
2 teaspoons hot mustard

1   Slice the scallops in three horizontally, then cut each slice in half crosswise. If you are
using queen scallops, slice them in two horizontally.

2   Put the dried chrysanthemum or the flower petals in a strainer. Pour hot water from a
kettle all over, and leave to drain. When cool, gently squeeze the excess water out. Set
aside and repeat with the watercress.

3   Mix together all the ingredients for the dressing in a bowl. Add the scallops
5 minutes before serving and mix well without breaking them. Add the flower petals and
watercress, then transfer to four bowls. Serve cold. Add a little more *shoyu*, if required.

cook's tips

• Any white fish sashimi can be used in this dish in place of the scallops.
• Replace the watercress with the finely chopped green part of scallions.
• Do not pick chrysanthemums from your garden for this salad, as the edible species are
  different to ornamental ones. Fresh edible chrysanthemums and other edible flowers
  are sometimes available from large supermarkets, or look for dried ones, called *kiku
  nori*, in Asian stores.

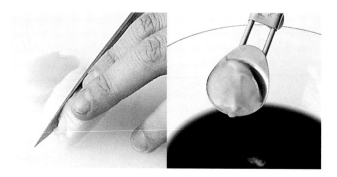

sake to avocado no o-sashimi salad

A MARINADE OF LEMON AND *DASHI-KONBU* "COOKS" THE SALMON IN THIS DISH, WHICH IS THEN SERVED AS PART OF A RICHLY FLAVORED AVOCADO AND *SHISO* SALAD.

1   Cut one of the salmon fillets in half crosswise at the tail end where the fillet is not wider than 1½ inches. Cut the other, wider part in half lengthwise. This means the fillet is cut into three. Cut the other salmon fillet in the same way.

2   Pour the lemon juice and two of the *dashi-konbu* pieces into a wide, shallow plastic container. Lay the salmon pieces in the container and sprinkle with the rest of the *dashi-konbu*. Leave to marinate for 15 minutes, then turn once and leave for 15 minutes more. The salmon should change to a pink "cooked" color. Remove the salmon from the marinade and wipe with paper towels. Reserve the marinade. Holding a very sharp knife at an angle, cut the salmon into ¼-inch-thick slices against the grain.

3   Cut the avocado in half, and sprinkle with a little of the reserved marinade. Remove the avocado pit and skin, then cut into ¼-inch-thick slices.

4   Mix the *miso* mayonnaise ingredients in a small bowl. Spread about 1 teaspoon onto the back of each of the *shiso* leaves, then mix the remainder with 1 tablespoon of the remaining salmon marinade to loosen the mayonnaise.

5   Arrange the *shiso* leaves on four plates. Top with the avocado, salmon, salad leaves and almonds, and drizzle over the remaining *miso* mayonnaise.

6   Alternately, you can build a tower of avocado and salmon slices. For each serving, take an eighth of the avocado slices and arrange them in the center of a plate, slightly overlapping. Add a *shiso* leaf, *miso*-side down, then place the same number of salmon slices on top, again slightly overlapping. Repeat the process. Arrange the salad leaves and almonds around the tower, and spoon the *miso* mayonnaise here and there on the plate. Serve immediately.

SERVES FOUR

9 ounces very fresh salmon tail, skinned and filleted
juice of 1 lemon
4-inch *dashi-konbu*, wiped with a damp cloth and cut into 4 strips
1 ripe avocado
4 *shiso* leaves, stalks removed and cut in half lengthways
about 4 ounces mixed salad leaves such as corn salad, frisée lettuce or arugula
3 tablespoons sliced almonds, toasted in a dry frying pan until just slightly browned

For the *miso* mayonnaise

6 tablespoons good quality mayonnaise
1 tablespoon *shiro miso*
ground black pepper

maguro butsu

THIS DISH OF CURED AND MARINATED RAW TUNA IS ONE OF THE EASIEST SASHIMI DISHES TO PREPARE AND IS READY TO EAT IN UNDER 20 MINUTES.

SERVES FOUR

14 ounces very fresh tuna, skinned
1 carton mustard and cress, roots
     cut off (optional)
4 teaspoons *wasabi* paste from a
     tube, or the same amount of
     wasabi powder mixed with
     2 teaspoons water
4 tablespoons *shoyu*
8 scallions, green part only,
     finely chopped
4 *shiso* leaves, cut into thin
     slivers lengthwise

1 Cut the tuna into ¾-inch cubes. If using mustard and cress tie into pretty bunches or arrange as a bed in four small serving plates or bowls.

2 Just 5–10 minutes before serving, blend the *wasabi* paste with the *shoyu* in a bowl, then add the tuna and scallions. Mix well and leave to marinate for 5 minutes. Divide among the plates or bowls and add a few slivers of *shiso* leaves on top. Serve immediately.

cook's tips
• Always buy perfectly fresh raw tuna from a reputable supplier, choosing a chunky piece without veins.
• The portion given here is known as *tsumami*, or nibble size. Usually, two or three different *tsumami* are served together as a first course. If served alone, add avocado to make a more filling dish. Peel and remove the pit from a large avocado, then cut the flesh into pieces that are roughly the same size as the tuna. Arrange the tuna and avocado cubes in a mosaic pattern on a plate or in a bowl.

SUSHI AND SASHIMI MADE EASY

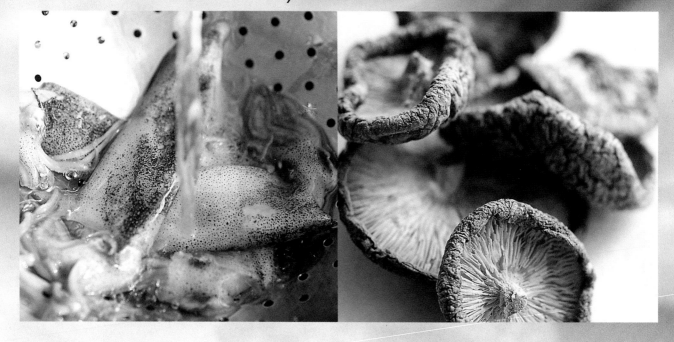

THERE'S NO REASON TO BE SCARED of sushi or sashimi. You need little by way of specialist equipment, the ingredients are easy to come by, and the basic techniques are not difficult to master. Start by making simple pressed sushi, then try your hand at *hoso-maki*, those pretty little rolls wrapped in *nori*. As your confidence increases, advance to hand-molded shapes. Sushi is an art form, open to interpretation by the individual, so don't feel that you have to compete with the experts. The same is true of sashimi. Find yourself a first-class supplier of fresh fish, practise in the privacy of your own kitchen, and you'll soon be at the cutting edge.

equipment

YOU DON'T NEED ELABORATE EQUIPMENT TO MAKE SUSHI OR SASHIMI. GOOD, SHARP KNIVES AND A DECENT CHOPPING BOARD ARE ESSENTIALS, AND YOU'LL NEED A SUSHI ROLLING MAT (*MAKISU*) TO MAKE ROLLED SUSHI, BUT BEYOND THAT, EVERYTHING YOU WILL REQUIRE WILL BE FOUND IN ANY REASONABLY WELL-EQUIPPED KITCHEN.

chopping boards

If you cut ingredients properly, you are assured of success in Japanese cooking, and the chopping board becomes your stage. The Japanese word for chef, *itamae*, means "before the board", and in Japan, no food preparation is done without a suitable board. Professional sushi chefs prefer cutting on wood, which is kinder to knives, but many home cooks choose washable plastic boards, thought by many to be more hygienic. Whatever type of board you use, it is very important to wash it thoroughly after every use. Different ingredients, particularly raw fish and meat, should never be placed on a board at the same time. If you make sashimi regularly, it is worth keeping a board specifically for this purpose.

hashi

In contrast to the many items of earthenware in a Japanese kitchen, the only cutlery you are likely to encounter are *hashi*. Shorter and more delicate than Chinese chopsticks, *hashi* (or more politely, *ohashi*) have pointed ends and come in several sizes. Men's *hashi* are thicker and usually slightly longer than women's, and there are children's sizes as well. *Hashi* have pointed ends and are made of various woods, lacquered bamboo, and plastic.

In Japanese households, each family member usually has a pair for daily use in the home, with a second pair reserved for taking out with a lunch box. During meals, *hashi* should be placed crosswise on a *hashi* rest or on a dish, but never directly on the table. The *hashi* rest is a small narrow boat-shaped piece of wood, porcelain, lacquer or metal, about 2 inches long. *Hashi* rests are also made in different, decorative shapes, such as ovals and birds.

Some *hashi* are extremely beautiful, but appearance and tradition are not the only reasons for using them. Food eaten with cutlery can acquire a slight metallic taste. Fish, especially marinated fish, tastes much better when eaten with *hashi*.

knives

When buying kitchen knives, it pays to buy the best you can afford. This holds good for whatever you are cooking, but is particularly valid when preparing sushi or sashimi. A professional sushi chef regularly uses at least 20 types of knife, but for the amateur enthusiast, a good set of standard kitchen knives will suffice for sushi. If you intend to make sashimi regularly it is well worth investing in a special sashimi knife. This is normally about 12 inches long, with a very sharp blade which does not taper, but maintains more or less the same width along its length.

If you are buying a set of knives specifically for making sushi, seek advice from the staff at a specialist Japanese shop. Many Japanese knives have a single sharp edge on one side of the blade only, which makes them thinner than most Western equivalents. This makes them perfect for delicate cutting and carving.

The finest Japanese knives are produced, like swords, from a single piece of carbonized steel. The blades are hard and smooth, and will take and keep a keen cutting edge. They must be looked after carefully, as they are liable to stain and rust if not washed and dried immediately after use. Stainless steel and ground mixed steel are both popular choices for domestic kitchens.

Sharpen your knives regularly, and keep them in a knife block, on a special rack or in separate compartments in a drawer.

pans

To make *su-meshi*, the vinegared rice that is the basis of all kinds of sushi, you will need a heavy pan with a tight-fitting lid. Where rice is steamed, then mixed with beans, as when making *sekihan*, a bamboo or stainless steel steamer will prove useful, and this can also be employed for cooking vegetables or fish. You will also need a small frying pan for omelettes. Japanese cooks use a square or rectangular pan – *tamago-yaki-nabe* – for making rolled omelettes, but you can improvise by trimming a round omelette to the shape required.

rice cooker

Making sushi can be addictive. If it becomes a daily habit, it might be worth investing in a rice cooker. This electric appliance cooks rice perfectly and keeps it warm until you are ready to add the vinegar.

spatulas

Wooden spatulas are widely used in Japanese cooking and are handy for folding the vinegar mixture into cooked rice when making *su-meshi*. There are many types of Japanese rice spatulas, but the most popular ones are either bare or lacquered wood.

sushi rolling mat

The bamboo stick mat, known in Japanese as a *makisu*, is an essential tool for making both thick and thin *nori-maki* (sushi rolled in a seaweed sheet). The mat can also be used for other purposes, such as squeezing water out of cooked salad vegetables before they are dressed. There are two types of *makisu*. The first measures about 9 x 8 inches. It is made from linked bamboo sticks and has a flat side that is pale green and shiny. It is used primarily for rolling sushi. A slightly larger *makisu* is also used for rolling thick omelettes. It has triangular or rounded bamboo sticks that are threaded together to make a pattern, which is imprinted on the omelette roll. After use, sushi mats must be washed carefully to remove any food stuck between the sticks, then left to dry completely before storing.

sushi tub

The *handai* or *hangiri* is a fairly shallow wooden tub used for mixing *su-meshi* (vinegared rice). It is almost always made of Japanese cypress, which is porous. The wide base helps to speed up the cooling process, while the wood absorbs excess moisture, ensuring that the vinegared rice has just the right degree of stickiness and gloss. The sushi tub must be thoroughly soaked in cold water before use. Just before mixing the *su-meshi*, the water is drained off and the sushi tub is wiped with a cloth dampened with vinegar mixture. This stops the water that has been absorbed by the wood from making the sushi rice soggy.

If you make sushi often, a wooden tub is very useful, not only for mixing, but also for serving. An ordinary large china or glass mixing bowl can be used instead, but avoid using metal bowls, which will spoil the flavor of the rice. Sushi tubs are available from specialist Japanese stores.

wooden molds

If you make *oshi-zushi* (pressed sushi) regularly, you may want to buy a traditional, rectangular wooden mold. These come in various sizes and, like the sushi tub, need to be soaked in water before use. Alternately, you can improvise by using a rectangular plastic freezer box (10 x 3 x 2 inches is a good size) or even a loaf pan lined with plastic wrap. Small tea or coffee cups and egg cups can also be used, either as molds or to help with hand-shaping the rice, as when making *onigiri*.

ingredients

WHEN YOU ARE MAKING SUSHI FOR YOUR OWN PLEASURE AND FUN, THE CHOICE OF INGREDIENTS IS LIMITED ONLY BY YOUR IMAGINATION. CLASSIC SUSHI CONSISTS OF VINEGARED RICE WITH VARIOUS TOPPINGS, USUALLY RAW FISH THAT IS ABSOLUTELY FRESH, OR WHICH HAS BEEN BLANCHED OR MARINATED.

rice

Fundamental to sushi making is vinegared rice (*su-meshi*). This is freshly cooked rice that has been cooled swiftly while being encouraged to absorb a sweetened and salted vinegar mixture.

uruchimai The type of Japanese rice that is most commonly used for sushi is *uruchimai*, the short grain Japanese *Oryza sativa japonica*. Once cooked, it becomes quite tender and moist, but the rice remains just firm enough to retain a little crunchiness. Unlike long grain rice, *uruchimai* is slightly sticky when cooked, and it is this quality that makes it perfect for molding. Its rich, slightly sweet flavor is enhanced by the addition of the vinegar, sugar and salt solution that is added to make *su-meshi* (vinegared rice).

There are over three hundred types of short grain rice grown in Japanese paddy fields. Brand names such as Koshihikari and Sasanisiki are among the most popular. Other countries are also important producers, however, and most of the sushi rice that is sold in the West comes from California or Spain. Familiar Californian brands include Kahomai, Nishiki, Maruyu and Kokuho, while Spain produces Minori.

genmai This brown rice is less polished than the white rice types. Only the husk is removed, and it retains its bran and germ. *Genmai* is the most nutritious Japanese rice and is high in fiber, but it takes considerably longer to cook than white rice and is very chewy. Most chefs prefer to use the classic white sushi rice, which looks so good with a black nori wrapper or a colorful topping, but some sushi bars, particularly in California, offer short grain brown rice sushi too.

mochigome This short, opaque grain, sometimes known as glutinous rice, is very sticky and dense when cooked. *Mochigome* has a high sugar content, and is often steamed rather than boiled. This is the type of rice that is commonly used to make rice cakes and rice crackers, and is an important ingredient in making *mirin*, the Japanese sweet rice wine. Its use in sushi is limited to a few dishes, such as *sekihan*, which is a mixture of adzuki beans and rice in *kashiwa* (salted oak) leaves. In some regions, *mochigome* is mixed with short grain rice to make a stickier *su-meshi* that is easier to mold by hand.

storing rice

Rice tastes best when newly harvested, and then it gradually deteriorates. Although it keeps for a long time, it is best eaten as soon as possible. Transfer raw rice to an airtight container and keep it in an airy, cool place away from direct sunlight. Keep rice dry or it will soon turn moldy.

fish and shellfish

For sushi and sashimi, it is vital to use fish that is absolutely fresh. Always buy from a reputable source with a high turnover, stressing what the fish is to be used for, and prepare it as soon as possible after purchase. Some suppliers offer ready-sliced fish for sashimi, but it is better to buy the fish in one piece and slice it yourself just before serving. Not all fish used for sashimi is raw: it may be "cooked" in lemon juice, lightly seared, salted or blanched. The following are some of the most popular types of fish and shellfish used for sushi and sashimi:

saba (mackerel) Fresh mackerel has a delicious, succulent flavor, but quite a fishy smell, which is moderated when it is salted, as in *saba-zushi*. Mackerel also goes well with *miso* and vinegar. When served as sashimi, slices of mackerel are often dipped in a little *shoyu* mixed with grated fresh root ginger. It is imperative to use mackerel on the day it is caught, as it goes off very quickly. Smoked mackerel is also a popular ingredient.

ebi (shrimp) Large jumbo shrimp are widely appreciated for their shape and flavor. In Japan, very fresh shrimp are eaten raw, but they may also be cooked in boiling water for just long enough to turn red. Cooking them makes them curl up, so they are often carefully skewered first so that they remain straight.

sake (salmon) In the West, fresh raw salmon is sometimes used for sashimi, but not in Japan, due to the risk of parasite infestation. To use salmon in sashimi, ask a good fishmonger to cut you a chunk from a large salmon; do not use ready-cut steaks. Very fresh salmon is used in *tamaki-zushi* and in *sake to avocado no o-sashimi salad*, while salted salmon is an ingredient in *onigiri*. Smoked salmon is often used for sushi. It can either form a filling or topping, or take the place of *nori* when making rolled sushi.

hotate-gai (scallops) The coral, black stomach and frill must be removed from scallops before they are used for sashimi. The scallops look very pretty when sliced almost but not completely in half, so that when opened up they resemble butterflies.

ika (squid) Fresh raw squid is used for sashimi only when it is very fresh. Both the body and the tentacles are frequently used. Cutting the skinned body lengthwise, then crosswise into thin strips helps to reduce its chewy texture. The skin is frequently scored.

me-kajiki (swordfish) With its attractive pale pink flesh and excellent flavor, swordfish is popular for sashimi. For *kajiki no tataki* salad, it is cut against the grain.

toro or akami (tuna) One of the most popular fish in Japan, tuna is used for sushi and sashimi and is now widely available in the West. As with any fish for these dishes, it must be very fresh – avoid any that is discolored and remove any veins from the fish before using. Tuna is classified according to the part of the fish it comes from, and its oiliness. *Toro* tuna is from the lower part of the fish and is oilier than *akami*, which is the red meat from the upper part.

karei (turbot) For sashimi, turbot needs to be cut quite thickly. It tastes wonderful in a salad with a light *wasabi* dressing. The flesh should be creamy white – do not buy fish with a blue tinge. Brill, halibut, porgy and fillets of sole make good substitutes.

ikura (salmon roe) Golden-colored salmon roe is used to decorate sushi. The little eggs look pretty with snow peas on dishes such as *chirashi*. Salmon roe has already been salted to preserve it, so it normally keeps for a short time. It is widely available in jars at good delicatessens and at fish counters in some larger supermarkets.

vegetables

In sushi, vegetables play a supporting role in fillings and as decoration. Sashimi is sometimes served in exquisite salads, with fresh ingredients such as daikon, carrot, asparagus, cucumber and leaves of all types.

cucumber Thin strips of cucumber are often used as part of the vinegared rice filling in rolled sushi. Japanese cucumbers are smaller than Western ones, but the flavor is quite similar, so ordinary salad cucumbers make a good substitute.

daikon This long, white vegetable, also known by the Indian name *mooli*, is a member of the radish family. It is one of the most versatile vegetables and can be cooked in soup, chopped for salad, shredded for a sashimi garnish or grated finely for use as a condiment. It is also pickled to make *takuan* – bright yellow pickles often used for *nori*-rolled sushi. There are numerous varieties of daikon, in different shapes, sizes and hues. The most common one looks rather like a large parsnip, but with a pale green section at the top.

The flavor resembles that of radish, but it is not as pungent. When buying daikon for sushi or sashimi, choose firm, dense vegetables with shiny, undamaged skin. Peel them before use.

chrysanthemum leaves
These pretty zigzag leaves come not from the garden chrysanthemum, but from an edible variety of the plant. They are sometimes sold in specialist grocery stores and are worth looking out for, as they have an intense aroma and are delicious in salads. Try them in *hotate kobachi*, where they are mixed with watercress and fresh succulent scallops. Dried petals, called *kiku nori*, are sold in sheets in Asian stores.

seaweed

Several types of seaweed are used in Japanese cooking. They are all a good source of vegetable protein as well as vitamins and minerals.

konbu There are many varieties of this giant kelp. They are all dried and graded, classified by their uses, either for eating as is or for cooking. As its name suggests, *dashi-*

konbu is used for making *dashi*, the *bonito* tuna stock that is widely used in Japanese cooking.

nori Where would sushi be without sheets of this wafer-thin, dark-colored dried seaweed? It is most familiar as a covering for rolled sushi, but is also cut into strips and used for decoration. The sheets are dark green to black in color, and are almost transparent in places. The ones used for rolling sushi usually measure 8 x 7 inches and are sold in packets of five or ten. Mini *nori* sheets, about 3½ x 1¾ inches, are also usually available in larger Asian stores.

Although it has a light, smoky flavor, *nori* is mainly appreciated for its subtle ocean aroma. Dark, shiny *nori* has more flavor than the cheaper reddish types.

Toast *nori* on both sides before use, by gripping a sheet with tongs and holding it horizontally over a low heat until it is crisp and gives out an aroma. It will be very crisp within 10 seconds. Do not broil it. Ready-toasted nori – *yaki-nori* – is also available. When using a sheet of toasted *nori* to roll sushi, place it

shiny-side down on the *makisu* (sushi rolling mat).

tofu

Highly nutritious and low in fat and sugar, tofu is one of Japan's most important foods. It is made from processed soya beans. There are several forms, including firm tofu (*momen-goshi*) and silken tofu (*kinu-goshi*), but the most useful in terms of sushi-making is *abura-age*, a thin, deep-fried version.

abura-age The unusual feature of this form of tofu is that it can be slit open like pitta bread and then stuffed with vegetables and sushi rice to make dishes such as *inari-zushi*. *Abura-age* is very easy to use. The pieces are boiled in water for 1 minute, then drained, refreshed under cold running water and drained again. When cool, the pieces of tofu are squeezed to remove the excess moisture before being halved and gently eased open. The "bags" are then simmered in a little *dashi* stock before being filled. *Abura-age* is available fresh, frozen and canned from most larger Japanese food stores.

flavorings and accompaniments

Sushi and sashimi are often garnished with *shiso* leaves. *Shoyu*, Japanese soy sauce, is a classic accompaniment, as are *gari*, paper-thin, pretty pink slices of pickled ginger. *Wasabi* turns up the heat, encouraging you to reach for your glass of sake.

gari Sushi and sashimi are always accompanied by *gari* – pickled ginger slices. Not only do the pretty pink ginger slices taste delectable, their piquant flavor also serves to cleanse the palate between mouthfuls. When you are sampling more than one type of sushi, it is traditional to eat a slice or two of gari between tastings. *Gari* can be bought ready-prepared in jars, but it is quite easy to make your own.

rice vinegar The aroma of Japanese rice vinegar is mild and sweet, and is not as sharp as distilled white vinegar or wine vinegar. Its subtle acidic flavor dissipates quickly, so it should be added to dishes at the last moment. Pure rice vinegar is labelled *yonezu*. *Kokumotsu-su* is a cheaper version, which includes other grains. Rice vinegar has numerous applications. It is used with sugar and salt to make *su-meshi* (vinegared rice) and is used for curing raw fish, as in the recipe for *saba-zushi*. When you are shaping sushi by hand, it helps to dip your hands in water mixed with a little rice vinegar, as this prevents the rice sticking to your fingers.

sake The classic drink to serve with both sushi and sashimi, this is a colorless rice wine. It has a fragrant aroma and subtle flavor.

shiso There are two types of this herb, green and red (commonly known as the beefsteak plant in the United States). The whole *shiso* plant, from berries to flowers, is used as a herb or garnish for Japanese dishes. Green *shiso* is used both as a herb and a garnish for sashimi and vinegared salads. It has a quite distinctive, pungent aroma and a rich, subtly piercing flavor. Buy the green leaves in packets from Asian stores. Store them in a plastic bag in the refrigerator and use within three days.

shoyu Japanese soy sauce is without doubt the single most important ingredient in the nation's cuisine. It is made from *dais* (soya beans), wheat and salt. There are two basic types: *usukuchi* (light) and *koikuchi* (dark). *Usukuchi* is an all-purpose sauce, clearer but saltier than *koikuchi*, which is used when making sauces, such as that used in teriyaki. *Shoyu* is often used on its own as a dip for sushi and sashimi. Don't be tempted to dunk the sushi in a large bowl of *shoyu*, or it will become too salty. Pour 1–2 tablespoons into a small sauce dish and use it sparingly.

wasabi This flavoring has trapped many an unwary diner. The pale green color gives it an innocuous appearance, but the taste is fiery in the extreme. *Wasabi* is sometimes referred to as Japanese horseradish, but the only connection it has with that plant is that both are roots. Freshly grated *wasabi* is a rarity, even in Japan, and the root is more commonly sold as a powder, which is mixed with tepid water to make a paste. Like mustard, this should be left to stand for about · 10 minutes before being used, to allow the sharp flavor to develop. *Wasabi* is also sold ready-prepared in tubes, like tomato paste, but is a lot more powerful than mustard.

techniques

ACQUIRING THE ARTISTRY AND SKILL OF A MASTER CHEF TAKES YEARS, BUT LEARNING A FEW BASIC TECHNIQUES WILL SET YOU ON THE PATH TO SUCCESS WITH SUSHI AND SASHIMI.

Making *su-meshi*

Su-meshi – vinegared rice – is the basis for all kinds of sushi. Short grain rice is soaked in water, then cooked by the absorption method before being mixed with vinegar, sugar and salt. The proportions of these ingredients vary, according to the whim of the chef and the way in which the rice is to be used. The basic recipe below should be followed whenever a recipe in this book calls for 1 quantity of *su-meshi*. When more *su-meshi* is called for, it may be necessary to adjust the amount of sugar.

1 Wash 7 ounces|1 cup Japanese short grain rice thoroughly in cold water. When the water runs clear, drain the rice well and set aside for 1 hour.

2 Put the rice into a deep pan and add 9 fluid ounces| 1⅛ cups water. The level of the water should not be more than a third of the depth of the pan.

3 Cover the pan, place over a high heat and bring to the boil. Cook for 5 minutes, then turn the heat to the lowest setting and simmer the rice for 7–13 minutes, or until the water has been absorbed. Remove the pan from the heat and set aside, still covered, for 10 minutes.

4 Meanwhile, in a small bowl, mix together 3 tablespoons Japanese rice vinegar with 7½ teaspoons sugar and 2 teaspoons coarse salt. Tip the cooked rice into a wet wooden sushi tub or a mixing bowl. Sprinkle with the vinegar mixture.

5 Using a wooden spatula, gently fold the vinegar mixture into the rice. Do not stir. Cooling the rice at the same time, by fanning it, helps to ensure perfect results. Cool before shaping, but do not chill or the rice will harden.

Shaping and topping sushi

Su-meshi (vinegared rice) can be shaped in a mold, by hand or by being rolled.

1 With wet hands, scoop about 1½ tablespoons *su-meshi* into your palm. Mold it into a rectangular block. Do not squash the rice, but ensure that the grains stick together.

2 Take a piece of the chosen topping and rub a little *wasabi* paste in the middle of it. Top with the *su-meshi* block and press it in place.

Making rolled sushi

1 Cover a *makisu* (sushi rolling mat) with a toasted sheet of *nori*, placed shiny side down.

2 Spread the *su-meshi* evenly over the nori, leaving a ½-inch margin on the side farthest from you. Press the rice down firmly.

3 Spread a thin strip of *wasabi* paste lengthwise down the center of the rice and arrange the filling horizontally over it.

4 Roll up the *makisu* from the near side. Squeeze gently to firm the filled *nori* roll, then carefully unwrap the mat. Put the roll on a slightly dampened wooden board and cover with plastic wrap. Slice in small pieces just before serving.

slicing fish for sashimi

Perfect, professional sashimi requires great artistry, but these simple sashimi cuts are good for beginners.

Slicing turbot

1 Place the fillet skinned side down. With the knife almost horizontal, shave the fish very thinly across the grain.

Slicing tuna

1 Cut a large chunk of fresh tuna into rectangular fillets about 1 inch thick and 2¼ inches wide.

2 For sashimi, slice the fish into ½-inch-thick pieces. Remember to keep the blade at a slight angle as you cut the fish.

3 For sushi, cut across the grain into ¼-inch-thick slices, keeping the blade at an angle to the board.

Cooking straight shrimp

Very fresh shrimp can be eaten raw, but cooking brings out the color.

1 Insert a bamboo skewer or toothpick into each shrimp lengthwise to keep it straight. Boil in salted water for 2 minutes.

2 Drain. When cool, remove the skewers and remove the black vein from each shrimp. Cut the shrimp almost through from the belly side, then open out flat to serve.

Making pickled ginger

1 Peel 7 ounces ginger root. Rub with 1–2 teaspoons salt, the set aside for 24 hours.

2 Pour 8 fluid ounces|1 cup rice vinegar into a bowl and add 4 fluid ounces|½ cup water. Stir in 3 tablespoons sugar until completely dissolved.

3 Rinse and drain the ginger. Add to the vinegar mixture and marinate for 1 week. Slice thinly as needed.

Making *dashi* stock

Dashi stock is the flavoring that underpins so many Japanese dishes. Second *dashi* stock is an all-purpose stock, while first *dashi* stock is more delicate in flavor and is best used for light dishes.

1 Pour 1 pint|2½ cups water into a pan and add a 4-inch piece of standard *konbu*. Leave to soak for 1 hour. Place, uncovered, over a medium heat and bring almost to boiling point.

2 Remove the *konbu*; reserve for the second dashi stock. Bring the water to the boil.

3 Add 4 tablespoons cold water to the pan with ¾-ounce or 3 x ⅛ ounce packets *kezuri-bushi*. Bring back to the boil, then remove the pan from the heat. Do not stir. Leave until the *kezuri-bushi* has completely settled on the base of the pan.

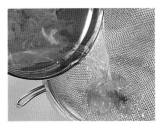

4 Strain through a fine strainer into a bowl, reserving the *kezuri-bushi* in the strainer to make a second *dashi* stock. The first *dashi* stock liquid is now ready for use.

5 To make second *dashi* stock, put the reserved *konbu* and *kezuri-bushi* from the first *dashi* stock into a pan with 1 pint|2½ cups water. Bring to the boil, then reduce the heat and simmer gently for about 15 minutes, or until the stock is reduced by roughly a third.

6 Add ½ ounce or 3 x ⅛ ounce packets *kezuri-bushi* to the pan and immediately remove it from the heat. Skim any scum from the surface and leave to stand for about 10 minutes. Strain.

cook's tips

• *Kezuri-bushi* are small dried *bonito* flakes. Look for them in Japanese stores.
• Freeze-dried granules called *dashi-no-moto* can be used to make a quick *dashi* stock, if preferred.
• *Dashi* stock can be frozen.

index